Local Government
BOARD
BUILDERS

AF903781

Social Services and Public Health: The Role of the Board of Commissioners

Kristi A. Nickodem

School of
Government

The School of Government at the University of North Carolina at Chapel Hill works to improve the lives of North Carolinians by engaging in practical scholarship that helps public officials and citizens understand and improve state and local government. Established in 1931 as the Institute of Government, the School provides educational, advisory, and research services for state and local governments. The School is also home to a nationally ranked Master of Public Administration program; a Law, Government, and Public Service minor beginning in academic year 2026–2027; the North Carolina Judicial College; and specialized centers focused on community and economic development, information technology, and environmental finance.

The School is the largest university-based local government training, advisory, and research organization in the United States. Its current catalog of faculty scholarship features more than 1,000 books, manuals, reports, articles, bulletins, teaching resources, and other print and online content related to state and local government. Faculty at the School offer close to 300 courses, webinars, and specialized conferences each year for more than 15,000 public officials. The School also produces the *Daily Bulletin Online* each day the General Assembly is in session, reporting on activities for members of the legislature and others who need to follow the course of legislation.

Visit sog.unc.edu or call 919.966.5381 for more information on the School's courses, publications, programs, and services.

Printed in the United States of America
30 29 28 27 26   1 2 3 4 5
ISBN 978-1-64238-145-0

About the Series

Local Government Board Builders offers local elected leaders practical advice on how to effectively lead and govern. Each of the booklets in this series provides a topic overview, and many offer specific tips on effective practice, worksheets, and reflection questions to help local elected leaders improve their work. The series focuses on common activities for local governing boards, such as selecting and appointing committees and advisory boards, planning for the future, making better decisions, improving board accountability, and effectively engaging stakeholders in public decisions.

Kimberly L. Nelson, Distinguished Professor in public administration and government at the UNC School of Government, is the series editor.

Other Books in the Series

How Are We Doing? Evaluating Manager and Board Performance, Kimberly L. Nelson, Second Edition, 2026

Strategic Planning for Elected Officials, Obed Pasha, Second Edition, 2025

Suggested Rules of Procedure for the Board of County Commissioners, Trey Allen, Fourth Edition, 2017

Suggested Rules of Procedure for a City Council, Trey Allen, Fourth Edition, 2017

Wicked Problems: What Can Local Governments Do?, Eric M. Reece and Maureen M. Berner, 2014

Handbook for North Carolina Mayors and Council Members, David M. Lawrence, 2013[1]

1. Revised, updated edition planned by Rebecca Fisher-Gabbard.

Local Government Budgeting: A Guide for North Carolina Elected Officials, Julie M. Brenman with Gregory S. Allison, 2013[2]

The Property Tax in North Carolina, Christopher B. McLaughlin, 2012

Getting the Right Fit: The Governing Board's Role in Hiring a Manager, Vaughn Mamlin Upshaw, John A. Rible IV, and Carl W. Stenberg, 2011[3]

Local Government Revenue Sources in North Carolina, Kara A. Millonzi, 2011[4]

Public Outreach and Participation, John B. Stephens, Ricardo S. Morse, and Kelley T. O'Brien, 2011

Working with Nonprofit Organizations, Margaret Henderson, Lydian Altman, Suzanne Julian, Gordon P. Whitaker, and Eileen R. Youens, 2010[5]

Creating and Maintaining Effective Local Government Citizen Advisory Committees, Vaughn Mamlin Upshaw, 2010

A Model Code of Ethics for North Carolina Local Elected Officials, A. Fleming Bell, II, 2010[6]

Leading Your Governing Board: A Guide for Mayors and County Board Chairs, Vaughn Mamlin Upshaw, 2009

Be sure to look for new and revised editions available in 2026 and 2027.

---

2. Revised, updated edition planned by Gregory Allison and William Rivenbark.
3. Revised, updated edition planned by Julie Beasley and Carl Stenberg.
4. Revised, updated edition planned by Rebecca Badgett.
5. Revised, updated edition planned by Teshanee Williams.
6. Revised, updated edition planned by Rebecca Fisher-Gabbard.

Acknowledgments

This book builds on the social services and public health scholarship of Aimee N. Wall, Jill D. Moore, Kirsten E. Leloudis, and John Saxon. The author is grateful for their valuable contributions to this field.

Contents

Introduction

In North Carolina, county governments play a significant role with respect to the provision and administration of social services and public health programs at the local level. Every county in North Carolina is required to have

- a local health department and department of social services, each of which must provide certain services and programs in the county;
- a local health director and director of social services; and
- a governing board for the local health department and the department of social services.

Many options are available under North Carolina law for how these departments are configured, who leads them, and which boards govern them. Each board of county commissioners is responsible for determining (1) the type of agency that will provide social services and public health in the county and (2) the type of governing board for that agency (or agencies). The organization and governance structure a county chooses will affect the hiring process for the agency director and agency staff, who are all recruited and hired at the local level. Beyond determining these structures, state law assigns some other responsibilities to every board of commissioners with respect to a county's social services and public health functions.

This book will provide a basic introduction to some issues and decisions around county social services and public health functions. For a more in-depth discussion of each of the topics discussed in this book, please see **Appendix A** for suggested reading materials. For a comparison of different types of local boards of health and boards of social services, please see **Appendix B** (public health) and **Appendix C** (social services).

Social Services and Public Health: The Bigger Picture

North Carolina's social services system and public health system each involve a substantial role for county governments, which must administer programs at the local level while complying with state laws, policies, and funding-related requirements. Both social services and public health depend on a complex mix of federal, state, and county funding for services. In addition to complicated funding streams, county social services and public health agencies must also navigate a complex array of federal and state laws related to the programs they administer at the local level.

Social Services in North Carolina

Social services programs address a range of economic and social problems that impair the ability of families and individuals to function and thrive in society. These problems include poverty, hunger and food insecurity, lack of medical care, homelessness, child abuse and neglect, abuse and neglect of vulnerable adults, and unemployment, among others.

Under the direction of a director of social services, each county department of social services administers dozens of different programs. Counties are mandated by state law to deliver many of these programs, including child protective services, adult protective services, and programs of public assistance established in Chapter 108A of the North Carolina General Statutes. Each of these mandated programs is subject to different federal or state rules regarding eligibility, confidentiality, administration, and funding. Counties also have authority to create and fund nonmandated social services programs.[1] The services and programs provided by each department of social services in North Carolina can be divided into two primary categories: economic services and social work services.

- Economic services, also referred to as public assistance programs, assist eligible people through monetary payments and other economic supports. This category includes programs such as the Supplemental Nutrition Assistance Program (SNAP, known as "Food and Nutrition Services" in North Carolina), Medicaid, Temporary Assistance for Needy Families (known as "Work First" in North Carolina), and the Low-Income Energy Assistance Program (LIEAP). Most economic services programs are *means-tested,* meaning that eligibility is determined based on a person's or family's income and resources.
- Social work services, on the other hand, are typically provided without regard to income. Social work services provided by a county department of social services include protecting children and vulnerable adults who are at risk of abuse or neglect, acting as a public guardian to individuals adjudicated incompetent by a court, and helping families navigate the licensing process for foster care and adoption.

North Carolina has adopted a county-administered, state-supervised social services system under which social services programs are *administered* primarily by county agencies under the *supervision* of various state-level entities. North Carolina is one of only a small number of states in which social services programs are directly administered by counties rather than by the state. North Carolina's "county-administered" model has implications for counties related to funding, governance, liability, staff, and program administration.

The North Carolina Department of Health and Human Services (NCDHHS) is the state agency that is responsible for supervising the administration of state and federal–state social services programs. This includes issuing policies, program manuals, guidance documents,

1. Chapter 153A, Section 255 of the North Carolina General Statutes (hereinafter G.S.). For more information, see Kristi Nickodem, *County Legal Authority to Fund Non-Mandated Social Services Programs*, Coates' Canons: NC Loc. Gov't L. Blog, https://canons.sog.unc.edu/blog/2023/06/06/county-legal-authority-to-fund-non-mandated-social-services-programs/.

and forms for use by local social services agencies in interpreting and implementing the various laws and regulations governing social services programs. NCDHHS also handles some administrative functions directly or through contracts with private vendors. In addition to creating policies and providing technical assistance, NCDHHS also has the authority to take corrective action in the event that a local social services agency is noncompliant with the law.[2]

Public Health in North Carolina[3]

The General Assembly has declared that the purpose of the state's public health system is "to ensure that all citizens in the State have equal access to essential public health services."[4] The system's mission is to promote and contribute to the highest level of health possible for the people of North Carolina by identifying and preventing or reducing community health risks; detecting, investigating, and preventing the spread of disease; promoting healthy lifestyles and a safe and healthful environment; promoting the accessibility and availability of quality health care services in the private sector; and providing health care services when they are not otherwise available.

North Carolina has a *decentralized* public health system in which the state and county governments each exercise legal authority to act to protect and promote public health and share responsibility for ensuring that public health services are available to all the state's residents. However, most public health service delivery occurs at the local level through local health departments.

Under the direction of the local health director, each local health department in North Carolina must provide food, lodging, and institutional permitting and sanitation inspection services; individual on-site water-supply permitting and sanitation inspection services; sanitary sewage collection, treatment, and disposal permitting and inspection services; communicable disease control; and vital records registration. There are

---

2. *See* G.S. 108A-74.

3. This summary is a condensed version of material from Jill D. Moore & Kirsten E. Leloudis, *Public Health, in* County and Municipal Government in North Carolina (Christopher B. McLaughlin ed., UNC School of Government, 2025).

4. G.S. 130A-1.1.

Table 1. Mandated Public Health Services in North Carolina (10A N.C.A.C. 46, § .0201–.0216)

Local health department must provide	Local health department must provide, contract for, or certify available
• Food, lodging, and institutional sanitation • Individual on-site water supply • Sanitary sewage collection, treatment, and disposal • Communicable disease control • Vital records registration	• Adult health • Home health • Dental public health • Maternal health • Child health • Family planning • Public health laboratory

Source: Jill D. Moore & Kirsten E. Leloudis, *Public Health, in* County and Municipal Government in North Carolina (Christopher B. McLaughlin ed., UNC School of Government, 2025).

other services that a local health department must either provide directly, contract with another entity to provide, or certify to the state's satisfaction that such services are available in the county from other providers. These services include adult health, home health, dental public health, maternal health, child health, family planning, and public health laboratory services. Mandated public health services are identified in Table 1.

Statewide public health activities and programs in North Carolina are carried out by several officials and agencies. The officials with primary responsibility for public health are the secretary of health and human services and the state health director. The principal agencies are the NCDHHS Division of Public Health, the Commission for Public Health, and the North Carolina Local Health Department Accreditation Board. Together, these individuals and agencies make and enforce statewide rules for public health programs, administer statewide public health programs and provide some direct services, oversee and provide technical assistance for local public health programs, distribute federal and state funds to local public health agencies, ensure that local public health agencies meet state law requirements for accreditation, and coordinate North Carolina's public health activities with other state and federal agencies.

Organization and Governance Structures for Social Services and Public Health

In North Carolina, state law provides many options for how a local health department and department of social services may be organized and governed. Each board of commissioners has authority to determine the organization and governance model for social services and public health within the county. Some options feature a single county department and board, while others involve joining together with other counties to form a regional department and board. Table 2 shows key differences between the various organization and governance models for social services, while Table 3 compares the models available for public health.

Single-County Options

Legislation enacted by the North Carolina General Assembly in 2012 authorized boards of commissioners to adopt different approaches to the organization and governance of county human services functions, including social services and public health.[1] This law allowed any board of commissioners to combine two or more county human services functions—such as social services and public health—into a single consolidated human services agency under the control of a human services director who is appointed and supervised by the county manager.[2] Separately, the law

1. S.L. 2012-126.
2. *See* G.S. 153A-77(b).

Table 2. Local Social Services Organization and Governance Options at a Glance

Organization	Governing Board	Board Members Selected by[a]	Director Appointed by	Employees
County DSS	County board of social services	Appointment (3 or 5)	Board	Subject to SHRA
County DSS	BOCC	Election	BOCC	Subject to SHRA
CHSA	Appointed CHS board	Appointment (up to 25)	County manager, with the advice and consent of the CHS board	SHRA optional
CHSA	BOCC[b]	Election	County manager, with the advice and consent of the BOCC	SHRA optional
Regional DSS	Regional board of social services	Appointment (12–18)	Board	Subject to SHRA

Note: SHRA = State Human Resources Act, BOCC = board of county commissioners, CHS = consolidated human services, CHSA = consolidated human services agency, DSS = department of social services.

[a] Numbers in parentheses represent the number of members on each appointed board.

[b] An advisory committee for public health must be appointed if the CHSA includes public health. The requirement for a health advisory committee applies only to counties that abolish their health boards after January 1, 2012. This amounts to an exception for Mecklenburg County, which abolished its health boards (a county board of health and subsequently a CHS board) before that date.

Source: Kristi A. Nickodem & Kirsten E. Leloudis, Consolidated Human Services Boards in North Carolina (UNC School of Government, 2025).

Table 3. Local Public Health Organization and Governance Options at a Glance

Organization	Governing Board	Board Members Selected by[a]	Director Appointed by	Employees
County health department	County board of health	Appointment (11)	Board	Subject to SHRA[b]
County health department	BOCC[c]	Election	BOCC	Subject to SHRA
CHSA	Appointed CHS board	Appointment (Up to 25)	County manager, with the advice and consent of the CHS board	SHRA optional
CHSA	BOCC[c]	Election	County manager, with the advice and consent of the BOCC	SHRA optional
District health department	District board of health	Appointment (15–18)	Board	Subject to SHRA[b]
Public health authority (single county)	Public health authority board	Appointment (7–9)[d]	Board	Not subject to SHRA[e]
Public health authority (multi-county)	Public health authority board	Appointment (7–11)[d]	Board	Not subject to SHRA[e]

Note: SHRA = State Human Resources Act, BOCC = board of county commissioners, CHS = consolidated human services, CHSA = consolidated human services agency, DSS = department of social services.

[a] Numbers in parentheses represent the number of members on each appointed board.

[b] G.S. 126-5(a)(2)(c).

[c] An advisory committee for public health must be appointed if the CHSA includes public health. The requirement for a health advisory committee applies only to counties that abolish their health boards after January 1, 2012. This amounts to an exception for Mecklenburg County, which abolished its health boards (a county board of health and subsequently a CHS board) before that date.

[d] G.S. 130A-45.1(b) allows a public health authority that intends to apply for federally qualified health center status to have a board with no fewer than nine and up to twenty-five members.

[e] G.S. 130A-45.12.

Source: Kristi A. Nickodem & Kirsten E. Leloudis, Consolidated Human Services Boards in North Carolina (UNC School of Government, 2025).

also allowed any board of commissioners to directly assume the powers and duties of a county board of social services or county board of health.[3]

Since the law changed in 2012, North Carolina counties have the following single-county options available for structuring their social services and public health functions (multi-county options are discussed separately at the end of this section).

Option 1: Separate Departments, Separate Appointed Governing Boards

- A **county department of social services** may be governed by a three- or five-member **appointed board of social services** (the number may be increased to five or decreased to three by the board of commissioners).[4] On a five-member board, two members are appointed by the board of commissioners, two members are appointed by the state Social Services Commission, and the fifth member is appointed by a majority vote of the other four members. Social services board members must be county residents, but there are otherwise no additional qualifications established by law for serving on the board of social services. An appointed board of social services has the sole authority to appoint, discipline, and dismiss the county director of social services.
- A **county health department** may be governed by an **appointed board of health**, which consists of eleven members who are all appointed by the board of commissioners.[5] The board of health must include one physician licensed to practice medicine in North Carolina, one licensed dentist, one licensed optometrist, one licensed veterinarian, one registered nurse, one licensed pharmacist, one county commissioner, one professional engineer, and three representatives of the general public.[6] An

3. G.S. 153A-77(a).
4. G.S. 108A-2.
5. G.S. 130A-35.
6. All members must be county residents. If the county cannot find qualified members in some of the professional categories, the law allows members of the general public (or qualified professionals from other counties) to serve instead. See G.S. 130A-35(b) for more details.

appointed board of health has the sole authority to appoint, discipline, and dismiss the county health director.

In these models, employees of the county department of social services and county health department are subject to the State Human Resources Act and the State Human Resources Commission rules for local governments.[7]

Option 2: Separate Departments with One or Both Departments Governed by the Board of County Commissioners

A board of county commissioners can directly assume the powers and duties of a governing board appointed by the board of commissioners or acting under and pursuant to the authority of the board of commissioners.[8] In the human services arena, these boards include a county board of health, a county board of social services, or a consolidated human services board.

A board of commissioners that abolishes the governing board for social services or public health takes on all the legal responsibilities of those boards. If the board of commissioners is governing a *nonconsolidated* county department of social services, this includes the responsibility to appoint, evaluate, discipline, and dismiss the county director of social services. Likewise, if the board of commissioners is governing a *nonconsolidated* county health department, it is responsible for appointing, evaluating, disciplining, and dismissing the county health director.

Serving as the board of health will also require the board of commissioners to be responsible for the board of health's other statutory powers and duties, including local public health rulemaking, setting fees for some public health services, and adjudication of certain disputes related to local health rules or health enforcement actions.[9] Whenever a board of commissioners decides to assume the powers and duties of a board of health, the board of commissioners is required to appoint an "advisory committee" for public health.[10] The advisory committee must include members representing all of the required categories of membership for a county board of health, which are found in Chapter 130A, Section 35 of the North Carolina General Statutes (hereinafter G.S.). A health advisory committee

7. *See* G.S. 126-5(a)(2).

8. G.S. 153A-77(a). However, there are limitations on this authority established by G.S. 153A-76.

9. *See* G.S. 130A-39.

10. G.S. 153A-77(a).

is advisory in nature only—it has no legal role in health department governance beyond providing advice to the board of commissioners on public-health-related issues and decisions.

If the board of commissioners assumes the powers and duties of the board of social services or board of health while keeping the health department and department of social services *separate* (i.e., not consolidated, as described in Options 3 and 4 below), then the employees of these departments remain subject to the State Human Resources Act. In other words, unlike consolidation, board of commissioner governance of one or both departments does not change anything about the status of each department's employees.

Option 3: Consolidated Human Services Agency Governed by an Appointed Consolidated Human Services Board

A consolidated human services agency (CHSA) is created when a board of commissioners consolidates two or more county human services functions into a single agency under the direct control of a human services director, who is appointed and supervised by the county manager.[11] In most (but not all) counties that have created a CHSA, the board of commissioners has consolidated social services and public health into a single agency. Some CHSAs include other human services functions, such as transportation, aging and adult services, or veterans' services.[12]

The most significant difference between a CHSA and a nonconsolidated county department of social services or health department is that the consolidated human services director is appointed (and dismissed) by the county manager, not by the agency's governing board.[13] The county manager must, however, receive the governing board's "advice and consent" before appointing someone to the director's role. The human services director also reports directly to the county manager, unlike a traditional county social services director or health director who reports solely to their governing board. The human services director may only hire CHSA staff with the approval of the county manager (no such approval or oversight is required under the nonconsolidated models).

---

11. G.S. 153A-77(b), (e).

12. *See* G.S. 153A-76 for some limitations on which county functions may be consolidated into a consolidated human services agency.

13. G.S. 153A-77(e).

The other key difference between a CHSA and a nonconsolidated county department of social services or county health department is that after consolidation, CHSA employees are no longer covered by the State Human Resources Act and instead become subject solely to county personnel policies.[14] This change occurs by default when the CHSA is first created, unless the commissioners affirmatively choose to keep CHSA employees under the State Human Resources Act.

One option for governance of a CHSA is an appointed consolidated human services (CHS) board.[15] The CHS board must be composed of no more than twenty-five members and all members must be residents of the county in which the CHSA is located. All members of the CHS board are appointed by the board of commissioners. More information on the process for forming the initial appointed CHS board is available in the "Procedure for Creating an Appointed CHS Board" section of this book.

The CHS board must include four people who are consumers of human services;[16] two physicians licensed to practice medicine in North Carolina (one of whom must be a psychiatrist); one county commissioner; and eight professionals, each with qualifications in one of these categories: one psychologist, one pharmacist, one engineer, one dentist, one optometrist, one veterinarian, one social worker, and one registered nurse. The board may also include "members of the general public representing various occupations."[17]

If a CHSA includes social services and public health, the CHS board assumes the legal powers and duties of the board of social services and the board of health. However, in the CHSA model, the CHS board is not responsible for appointing or dismissing the CHSA director. That authority lies with the county manager, though the manager must have the "advice and consent" of the CHS board for these decisions.

---

14. G.S. 153A-77(d).

15. G.S. 153A-77(c).

16. The term "human services" is not defined under state law, which means counties have some leeway to interpret the concept.

17. G.S. 153A-77(c). The board of commissioners may appoint a member of the CHS board to concurrently fill more than one category of membership if the member has the qualifications or attributes of more than one category of membership. For example, if a candidate for board membership is a registered nurse and a consumer of human services, that single individual could fulfill requirements for representation of both those categories on the board.

Option 4: Consolidated Human Services Agency Governed by the Board of Commissioners

Another option for governance of a CHSA is the board of commissioners serving directly as the governing board for the CHSA.[18] If the CHSA includes both public health and social services, this means the board of commissioners is responsible for any powers and duties assigned by law to the board of health and board of social services.

In this model, the structure of the CHSA is the same as described in Option 3. The consolidated human services director is appointed and dismissed by the county manager, not by the board of commissioners (though the manager must receive the board's advice and consent before appointing someone to the director's role). As with Option 3, the human services director reports directly to the county manager and may only hire CHSA staff with the approval of the county manager. CHSA staff are subject solely to county personnel policies and not to the State Human Resources Act, unless the board of commissioners explicitly chooses to keep employees under the State Human Resources Act.

If the CHSA includes public health and the board of commissioners serves directly as the governing board, the board of commissioners must appoint a health advisory committee to provide advice to the commissioners on decisions related to public health. An advisory committee is something entirely different from an appointed CHS board (described in Option 3). What is the difference between the *advisory committee* in Option 4 and the *appointed CHS board* in Option 3? By way of example, in a county with a CHSA that includes public health and is governed by an appointed CHS board, it is the *CHS board* that has the authority to adopt or repeal a local public health rule. The CHS board serves as the board of health and exercises the board of health's statutory public health rulemaking authority. In a county where the board of commissioners acts as the governing board for a CHSA that includes public health, it is the *board of commissioners* that has the authority to adopt or repeal a local public health rule, though it may seek advice on the rule from its public health advisory committee. If the board of commissioners acts as the governing board for a CHSA that includes public health, then it is the board of commissioners—not the advisory committee—that acquires the core powers and duties of the board of health, including rulemaking, fee-setting, and

18. G.S. 153A-77(a).

adjudication. Put differently, an appointed CHS board is the governing board for a CHSA (though its powers with respect to the director are different from those of a traditional board of health or board of social services), while a public health advisory committee has no legal role in agency governance beyond providing advice to the board of commissioners.

Option 5: Unique Configurations for Consolidation and Nonconsolidation

A county may create a CHSA (described in Option 3) that does not include *both* public health and social services, so long as the CHSA includes at least two county human services functions or departments. For example, a county might choose to include public health and veterans' services in its CHSA and have that CHSA governed by an appointed CHS board, while leaving the county department of social services separate (nonconsolidated) under its appointed county board of social services. As another example, a county might consolidate social services, transportation, and veterans' services into its CHSA and have that CHSA governed by the board of commissioners, while leaving the county health department separate (nonconsolidated) under its appointed county board of health.

Multi-County Options

For either public health or social services, counties may forego the single-county options and instead join together to form a single multi-county department.

- A **district health department** is a multi-county agency that provides local public health services for the residents of all counties in the district. The department may be created upon mutual agreement of the boards of county commissioners and boards of health of two or more counties. A district health department is governed by a single district board of health and administered by a single health director.[19]
- A **regional department of social services (DSS)** is a multi-county agency that provides social services programs to the

19. *See* G.S. 130A-36 through -40.

> residents of all counties within the region.[20] A regional DSS may be formed upon mutual agreement of each of the county boards of commissioners and local boards of social services involved. A regional DSS is governed by a single regional board of social services and administered by a single director of social services.[21] North Carolina counties have had authority to voluntarily join together to create a regional DSS since 2019, but to date no counties have elected to create one.

A district health department or a regional DSS is a "public authority" for purposes of the Local Government Budget and Fiscal Control Act, meaning each is a separate legal entity from the counties involved. These multi-county departments are subject to many of the same laws that apply to county departments (e.g., laws relating to public records, open meetings, and financial management), but they are not county departments and have no power to levy taxes. A district health department or regional DSS has its own director, governing board, staff, and budget—all separate from the counties that formed the multi-county agency.

Other Options for Public Health

At the time of this publication, every North Carolina county except one is served by a county health department, a CHSA that includes public health, or a district health department.[22] However, two other options are available under North Carolina law for how counties may organize and govern their

---

20. A regional DSS may incorporate all social services programs offered by the county departments of social services or it may include only a selected subset of programs and services. For example, a regional DSS could focus exclusively on adult services (such as adult protective services and guardianship), public assistance programs, child welfare services, or child support enforcement. If the regional DSS does not incorporate all social services programs that must be provided by counties, then each county in the region must continue to operate its own department (either a county DSS or a consolidated human services agency, along with its own governing board and director) to offer the mandated programs and services not provided by the regional DSS.

21. *See* G.S. 108A-15.7 through -15.10.

22. One other model exists in North Carolina—a hospital authority with a hospital authority board—but is only available to counties with a hospital authority that meets specific criteria and is, at this time, only utilized by Cabarrus County. *See* S.L. 1997-502.

local health departments, though they are rarely used. Counties can opt to create a single-county or multi-county public health authority (PHA) to provide public health services.[23] A PHA is a governmental entity that is independent of the county. To create a single-county PHA, both the board of county commissioners and the local board of health must adopt a joint resolution stating that it is in the interest of the public health and welfare to provide public health services to the community through a PHA. To create a multi-county PHA or join an existing PHA, the boards of county commissioners and local boards of health in all participating counties must adopt a similar joint resolution. A PHA, whether single- or multi-county, is governed by a PHA board and administered by a PHA director. A PHA board has unique powers that are distinct in some respects from those of a county or district board of health. A full list of the PHA board's powers may be found in G.S. 130A-45.3.

23. G.S. 130A-45.02.

Procedures for Changing the Organization or Governance Structure for Social Services or Public Health

If the board of commissioners decides to change its organization or governance model to one of the single-county options described in the previous section, it must follow certain steps. The process is different depending on whether the board of commissioners intends to serve as the governing board for an agency or have an appointed board instead.

Procedure for Assuming the Powers and Duties of a Board of Social Services, Board of Health, or CHS Board

If a board of commissioners plans to serve as the governing board for a county department of social services, a county health department, or a CHSA, it must first hold a public hearing on the matter.[1] The board of commissioners must give thirty days' notice of the public hearing in a newspaper having general circulation in the county and must follow any notice requirements that would generally apply to official meetings of the board under North Carolina's open meetings law.[2] Following the public hearing, the board of commissioners may adopt a resolution "assuming and

1. G.S. 153A-77(a).

2. *See generally* G.S. 143-318.12 (public notice requirements for official meetings of public bodies).

conferring upon the board of county commissioners all powers, responsibilities and duties" of the applicable governing board(s).[3]

If a board of commissioners decides to assume the powers and duties of a county board of health or a CHS board in a county where the CHSA includes public health, the commissioners must appoint an advisory committee for public health (described in more detail under Option 2 and Option 4 in the "Organization and Governance Structures for Social Services and Public Health" section).[4] There is no legal requirement to create a social services advisory committee when the board of commissioners assumes the powers and duties of a social services governing board. However, a board of commissioners has the *option* of appointing an advisory committee for social services, even though doing so is not required by law.

What if a board of commissioners that has assumed the powers and duties of one of these governing boards decides that it wants to *revert* to having an appointed board for the county department of social services, health department, or CHSA? The board of commissioners may revert to the appointed board governance model at any time by following the statutory procedures for appointing a county board of social services (see G.S. 108A-3, -5), a county board of health (see G.S. 130A-35), or a CHS board (see G.S. 153A-77(c)). The thirty days' notice and public hearing requirement described above does not apply when the board of commissioners is moving away from the commissioner governance model and appointing one of these boards instead.

Procedure for Creating a Consolidated Human Services Agency

The law does not require a public hearing prior to forming a CHSA with an appointed CHS board. The public hearing is only required if the board of commissioners intends to serve as the governing board for the CHSA. However, even if the commissioners intend to appoint a CHS board, holding a hearing to discuss the potential consolidation is a best practice, given that the creation of a CHSA is a significant change for the county and is likely to draw many questions from county residents and employees.

---

3. G.S. 153A-77(a).
4. *See id.*

The law does not explicitly require counties to create a CHSA through the use of a resolution, unless the board of commissioners is also assuming the powers and duties of the agency's governing board. Nonetheless, it is sensible and prudent for a board of commissioners to adopt a resolution when forming a CHSA. The resolution establishes and clarifies which county departments or functions are being consolidated into the CHSA. The language of the resolution forming the CHSA can also be used to clarify whether employees will remain subject to the State Human Resources Act or instead be subject solely to county personnel policies.[5] To date, every county in North Carolina that has created a CHSA has done so through a resolution.

When establishing a new CHSA, the county manager has authority to appoint the CHSA's director but may do so only with the advice and consent of the CHSA's governing board.[6] Because of this requirement, there is a logical sequence that should be followed when first establishing a new CHSA.

1. The board of commissioners adopts a resolution creating a CHSA. The resolution should state which county human services functions or departments will be consolidated into the CHSA and whether CHSA employees will be subject to the State Human Resources Act.
2. The board of commissioners appoints a CHS board or directly assumes the powers and duties of the agency governing board through a resolution. This process of nominating and appointing the initial CHS board is described below.
3. The county manager identifies a candidate for CHS director and seeks the advice and consent of the CHSA's governing board.
4. If the CHSA's governing board consents to the appointment, the county manager appoints the CHS director to lead the CHSA.

This order of events is significant under the law. The CHS director cannot be appointed before the CHSA has been created and the governing board

---

5. CHSA employees will be exempt from the State Human Resources Act by operation of law unless the board of commissioners explicitly elects to keep them subject to its provisions. G.S. 153A-77(d).

6. G.S. 153A-77(e).

is in place because the governing board must consent to the CHS director's appointment. The timing of the meeting is also important if the board of commissioners intends to serve as the agency's governing board, due to the notice and public hearing requirements. The board of commissioners could hold the public hearing, create the CHSA, and assume the powers and duties of the CHSA's governing board in the same meeting, but it would have to ensure that the public had at least thirty days' notice of that meeting.

Procedure for Creating an Appointed CHS Board

If the board of commissioners forms a CHSA and opts to have an appointed CHS board (instead of serving directly as the governing board for the CHSA), the board of commissioners must first create a nominating committee consisting of members of the current (preconsolidation) board of health and social services board, as well as of the board responsible for managing mental health, developmental disabilities, and substance abuse services in the county.[7] The nominating committee recommends members for the new CHS board, and the board of commissioners must make appointments based upon those recommendations. The board of commissioners may want to form this nominating committee prior to creating the CHSA. Alternatively, the board of commissioners could create the CHSA by resolution in a manner that becomes effective at a later date (i.e., several months after the resolution is adopted) and form the nominating committee in the interim period.

The nominating committee should present the board of commissioners with a slate of candidates for the CHS board who are county residents and fulfill the required categories of membership. After the initial board is appointed by the board of commissioners, the board of commissioners fills future vacancies on the CHS board based upon nominees presented by the members of the then-current CHS board.

---

7. G.S. 153A-77(c). The original version of the consolidation statute (G.S. 153A-77) authorized the inclusion of the area mental health, developmental disabilities, and substance abuse services authority in a CHSA. In that context, it was logical that the area authority board would be represented on the nominating committee, along with the boards of health and social services. Counties may no longer consolidate an area authority into a CHSA, but the nominating committee requirements in the statute were never altered to reflect that change.

In order to establish a uniform staggered-term structure for the CHS board when it is first created, the board of commissioners may appoint some CHS board members for less than a four-year term.[8] This will prevent all of the board's members from rolling off at the same time. The term length of each of the initial CHS board members is determined at the discretion of the board of commissioners, though it must always be four years or less. To maintain continuity and stability, the board of commissioners will likely want to ensure that at least some of the initial board members are appointed for a full four-year term.

The initial CHS board can include members of the preconsolidation board of health and social services board, provided that those individuals otherwise meet the membership qualifications described under Option 3 in the "Organization and Governance Structures for Social Services and Public Health" section. Including some preconsolidation board members could help to provide continuity in board operations when the CHS board is first formed. Moreover, some counties may be unable to fulfill all the required categories of membership for the CHS board without nominating and appointing some of the preconsolidation board of health members.

Recruitment for board service is a challenge for many counties across North Carolina, especially in light of the many professions that must be represented on the CHS board. If no county resident is available to serve in one of the professional positions, then that seat on the CHS board may remain temporarily vacant. The county should, however, continue to make diligent efforts to recruit CHS board members who will fulfill all of the required categories of membership.

8. G.S. 153A-77(c).

Serving Ex Officio as a Commissioner on an Appointed Board of Social Services, Board of Health, or CHS Board

In counties with an appointed board of health or CHS board, the board of commissioners is required to appoint a county commissioner to serve on the board.[1] In counties with an appointed board of social services, the board of commissioners has authority to appoint one individual to a three-member board or two individuals to a five-member board.[2] The board of commissioners is not required to appoint one of its own members to an appointed board of social services but often chooses to do so.

When the board of commissioners appoints one of its members to serve on the board of health, board of social services, or CHS board, it is an *ex officio* appointment.[3] This means that a county commissioner is considered to be serving on the appointed board as a part of the commissioner's duties as a commissioner and not as a separate public office. Accordingly, the county commissioner's ex officio service on an appointed board of social services, board of health, or CHS board does not "count" as a separate public office for purposes of the multiple-office-holding limit imposed by state law and the North Carolina Constitution.[4]

A county commissioner who serves ex officio on a county board of health or an appointed CHS board may only serve on the board for as long

1. G.S. 130A-35(b); G.S. 153A-77(c).
2. G.S. 108A-3.
3. G.S. 128-1.2.
4. N.C. Const. art. VI, § 9; G.S. 128-1.1.

as the member is a county commissioner.[5] However, the term of a county commissioner who serves ex officio on an appointed county board of social services is the same as other board members (a three-year term) and is not tied to the individual's term on the board of commissioners.[6]

---

5. G.S. 153A-77(c).
6. G.S. 108A-4; State *ex rel.* Pitts v. Williams, 260 N.C. 168 (1963).

Responsibilities of All Boards of Commissioners Regarding Social Services and Public Health

In some counties, the board of commissioners may serve directly as the governing board for social services or public health. But even in counties where the board of commissioners does *not* serve directly as the governing board for the county's department of social services, health department, or CHSA, the commissioners have a number of duties regarding social services and public health agencies, boards, and programs.

Duties Related to Funding and Compensation

- A primary role of the board of commissioners is ensuring the adequacy of funds for social services, public health, and other human services programs in the county budget.
- The board of commissioners is responsible for approving the compensation of all county employees, including the director of social services, health director, and other social services and public health staff.[1]
- The board of commissioners has authority to establish per diem rates and a policy for subsistence and travel reimbursement for members of the DSS board, county board of health, or CHS

1. G.S. 153A-92.

board.[2] If the board of commissioners establishes a per diem rate and a policy for reimbursement, it must also include funds in the county budget to cover such expenses.

Duties Related to Public Health Programs and Administration

- State law authorizes a county to "provide for and regulate the public health pursuant to Chapter 130A of the General Statutes and any other law authorizing local public health activities."[3] While the county is required to provide certain public health services, the board of commissioners can also use its authority to set the county budget to inform which *nonmandated* public health services the county will provide (if any).
- State law authorizes a board of commissioners to establish sanitary districts and mosquito control districts as necessary to protect and promote the public health.[4]
- A board of commissioners may also adopt ordinances to address "conditions detrimental to the health, safety, or welfare" and may abate public health nuisances.[5] However, any such ordinance does not apply to municipalities within the county and does not impede a local board of health's authority to adopt local rules to protect and promote the public health.[6] The relationship between the board of commissioners' ordinance authority and the local board of health's authority to engage in public health rulemaking is addressed in Chapter 8 of *Local Boards of Health in North Carolina*, by Kirsten E. Leloudis.

---

2. G.S. 108A-8 (DSS board); G.S. 130A-35(h) (board of health); G.S. 153A-77(c) (CHS board).
3. G.S. 153A-247.
4. G.S. 130A, art. 2, pt. 2 (sanitary district); G.S. 130A, art. 12, pt. 2 (mosquito control district). A sanitary district provides water and wastewater services to communities within its jurisdiction. A mosquito control district is responsible for managing populations of mosquitoes and other arthropods, which can be vectors for disease.
5. G.S. 153A, §§ 121, 140.
6. G.S. 153A, §§ 121(c), 122. The governing board of a municipality may, however, adopt a resolution permitting a county ordinance to be applicable within the municipality.

- State law authorizes each county board of health to set fees that are charged by the health department for certain public health services. The board of health must base its fees on a plan proposed by the health director (or human services director, in the CHSA model), and any fees adopted by the board of health must be approved by the board of commissioners (if the commissioners are not directly serving as the governing board for public health).[7] There are limits on the type of fees that a board of health may adopt and a local health department may charge for public health services, particularly in the realm of environmental health services.

Duties Related to Social Services Programs and Administration

- Every board of county commissioners is required by law to levy and collect taxes sufficient to meet its county's share of expenses for state-mandated social services programs.[8] If a county does not pay or arrange for payment of its full share of these costs, the state budget director is authorized to withhold from the county any state appropriations for public assistance and related administrative costs or to direct the secretary of revenue and the state controller to withhold specified tax revenues owed to the county. The state budget director must notify the chair of the board of commissioners of the proposed action prior to withholding any funds.[9]
- While state law requires counties to participate in a number of social services programs, it also authorizes counties to "undertake, sponsor, organize, engage in, and support other social service programs intended to further the health, welfare, education, employment, safety, comfort, and convenience of its citizens."[10] Through its power over the county budget, the board of commissioners has authority to determine what

7. G.S. 130A-39(g); G.S. 153A-77(d)(1).
8. G.S. 108A-90.
9. G.S. 108A-93.
10. G.S. 153A-255.

nonmandated social services programs the county will provide and has discretion as to how much county money to budget for those nonmandated programs.

- State law allows the board of commissioners, with the approval of the social services board (if the county has an appointed board of social services), to appoint an attorney as the "special county attorney for social service matters" or to designate a county attorney to serve in that role.[11] A county is not required to have a special county attorney for social services, but if it does, that attorney's duties include serving as legal adviser to the board of commissioners, the director of social services, and the CHS board regarding social services matters. The board of commissioners is also responsible for determining the attorney's compensation.
- State law requires counties to operate the State-County Special Assistance program, which is designed to assist needy aged or disabled persons in paying for room and board in adult care homes, special-care units, and in-home living arrangements. The board of commissioners has authority to determine whether this program will also provide financial assistance for a different category of "certain disabled persons" who are in private living arrangements but may not otherwise qualify for State-County Special Assistance under the eligibility requirements set forth in state law.[12]
- Each county must administer a child support enforcement program.[13] Most county child support enforcement programs are operated by a county department of social services

---

11. *See* G.S. 108A-16 through -18.

12. Per G.S. 108A-42, a "Certain Disabled" person is a person in a private living arrangement who is at least eighteen but younger than sixty-five, "having a physical or mental impairment which substantially precludes him from obtaining gainful employment, which impairment appears reasonably certain to continue without substantial improvement throughout his lifetime." By contrast, eligibility for State-County Special Assistance requires that the recipient meet certain income criteria, along with being (1) sixty-five years of age or older or (2) between the ages of eighteen and sixty-five and *permanently and totally* disabled or legally blind. G.S. 108A-41. Eligibility requirements for the "Certain Disabled Program" are set forth at Title 10A, Chapter 71P, Section .080 of the North Carolina Administrative Code (hereinafter N.C.A.C.).

13. G.S. 110-141.

or CHSA. However, each board of commissioners has the option of creating an independent county department for child support enforcement, locating the program in another county department or office, or contracting with a private entity or another county to operate the program.

- State law authorizes each board of social services to enter into contracts under which the department of social services will voluntarily render services in exchange for a fee.[14] Any fees charged by the board using this contract authority must be based on a plan that is developed by the DSS director and approved by the board of commissioners (and by the appointed board for social services, if the commissioners are not directly serving as the governing board for social services). An appointed board of social services is required to make an annual report to the county commissioners regarding receipt of such fees.

Duties Related to the Work First Program

The federal Temporary Assistance for Needy Families (TANF) program is called "Work First" in North Carolina and is administered by every county department of social services in North Carolina. Work First provides eligible families with short-term assistance to help them achieve self-sufficiency through employment. State law allows each board of commissioners to indicate to the North Carolina Department of Health and Human Services (NCDHHS) whether the county wants to be a "standard" or "electing" county for purposes of the Work First program.[15] In a "standard" county, NCDHHS is responsible for the development and supervision of the Work First program, which is administered by the county department of social services (or CHSA, if the CHSA includes social services).[16] In an "electing" county, the board of commissioners is directly responsible for the development, administration, and implementation of the Work First program.[17]

---

14. G.S. 108A-10; G.S. 153A-77(d).

15. G.S. 108A-27(e). When notifying NCDHHS of the county's desire to be designated as electing or standard, the county must submit documentation demonstrating that three-fifths of its county commissioners support the desired designation.

16. G.S. 108A-27.8(a).

17. G.S. 108A-27(f).

A board's request to become an electing county must be supported by a three-fifths vote of the commissioners. The General Assembly designates each county as either a standard county or an electing county based on recommendations from NCDHHS.[18]

An electing county has more authority to set eligibility criteria, payment levels, and other program features that the state sets for standard counties. In an electing county, the board of commissioners is responsible for

- establishing outcome and performance goals,
- establishing eligibility criteria,
- entering into Mutual Responsibility Agreements with Work First recipients,
- ensuring that services and resources are available to help participants comply with the agreements,
- monitoring compliance with those agreements,
- ensuring that participants engage in the required hours of work activities,
- developing and submitting to NCDHHS a biennial county Work First plan,
- developing and implementing an appeals process for the county's Work First program, and
- complying with all state and federal laws regarding the Work First program.[19]

A board of commissioners may delegate most of these responsibilities to other public or private entities, but the board ultimately remains accountable for all of them.

In electing counties, the board of commissioners must appoint a committee of individuals to identify the needs of the population to be served by Work First and to assist in developing the county's Work First plan to respond to those needs.[20] The committee membership must include, but is not limited to, individuals from the county board of social services (which may be a CHS board), the board of the area mental health authority, the local board of health, the local school systems, the business community, the board of commissioners, and community-based organizations representative of the population served by the Work First program.

18. G.S. 108A-27.2(12)–(14).
19. G.S. 108A-27.3.
20. G.S. 108A-27.3(c).

Conflicts of Interest for County Commissioners Related to Social Services

Under G.S. 14-234(a), county commissioners are prohibited from certain actions related to making and administering contracts on behalf of the county due to conflicts of interest. These prohibitions sometimes apply when commissioners (or their spouses) receive a direct benefit under a contract they are making or administering on behalf of the county, or when they are attempting to improperly influence any other government official who is involved in making or administering a contract on behalf of the county. Discussing those prohibitions is beyond the scope of this book, but some of the resources recommended in Appendix A provide more detailed information on this topic.

In addition to the conflicts of interest defined by G.S. 14-234(a), there are several unique conflicts of interest related to public assistance and social services that commissioners should keep in mind.

First, state law expressly prohibits payments being made under the State-County Special Assistance or Medicaid programs on behalf of persons who are residents or patients in adult care or nursing homes that are owned or operated, in whole or in part, by a county commissioner, a social services board member, or the spouse of a county commissioner or social services board member.[1]

Second, the county department of social services is prohibited from supervising county commissioners and social services board members as foster parents in the county in which they serve on the board.[2]

1. G.S. 108A, §§ 47, 55(d).
2. 10A N.C.A.C. 70E, § .1105.

Finally, commissioners should also be mindful of G.S. 14-234.3, which prohibits a county commissioner who serves as a director, officer, or governing-board member of a nonprofit organization from participating in making or administering any contracts between that nonprofit and the county. Specifically, commissioners who are directors, officers, or governing-board members of a nonprofit must recuse themselves from any deliberation or vote by the board of commissioners on a contract (including an award of money) with that nonprofit, and the recusal must be recorded with the board's clerk.

Appendix A. Recommended Reading

Boards of Health and Health Departments

Kirsten E. Leloudis, *Local Boards of Health in North Carolina* (UNC School of Government, 2025).

Jill D. Moore and Kirsten E. Leloudis, "Public Health," in *County and Municipal Government in North Carolina*, 2025 ed., edited by Christopher B. McLaughlin (UNC School of Government, 2025).

Boards of Social Services and Departments of Social Services

Kristi A. Nickodem, *Local Social Services Boards in North Carolina* (UNC School of Government, 2023).

Kristi A. Nickodem, "Social Services," in *County and Municipal Government in North Carolina*, 2025 ed., edited by Christopher B. McLaughlin (UNC School of Government, 2025).

Consolidated Human Services Boards and Agencies

Kristi A. Nickodem and Kirsten E. Leloudis, *Consolidated Human Services Boards in North Carolina* (UNC School of Government, 2025).

Kristi A. Nickodem, *Personnel Decisions for North Carolina's Consolidated Human Services Agencies*, Social Services Bulletin No. 49 (UNC School of Government, 2021), https://www.sog.unc.edu/publications/bulletins/personnel-decisions-north-carolinas-consolidated-human-services-agencies.

Ethics and Conflicts of Interest

Kristina M. Wilson and Crista M. Cuccaro, "Ethics and Conflicts of Interest," in *County and Municipal Government in North Carolina*, 2025 ed., edited by Christopher B. McLaughlin (UNC School of Government, 2025).

Other Electronic Resources

UNC School of Government, *Coates' Canons: North Carolina Local Government Law Blog*, https://canons.sog.unc.edu/. Navigate by "Categories" (see left navigation bar) to select posts about Public Health or Social Services.

The North Carolina Human Services Hub, humanservices.sog.unc.edu. This School of Government website provides up-to-date resources related to North Carolina's social services and consolidated human services agencies and boards, including a page featuring interactive maps of the state that reflect which counties have adopted various organization and governance models for social services and public health.

Appendix B. Comparisons of Local Boards of Health

Table B.1. Types of Local Boards of Health

Board	Organization	Board Members Selected by[a]	Director Appointed by
County board of health	County health department	Appointment (11)	Board
BOCC as board of health[b]	County health department	Election	BOCC
CHS board	CHSA	Appointment (Up to 25)	County manager, with the advice and consent of the CHS board
BOCC as CHS board[b]	CHSA	Election	County manager, with the advice and consent of the BOCC
District board of health	District health department	Appointment (15–18)	Board
Public health authority board	Public health authority	Appointment (7–9 for a single-county agency; 7–11 for a multi-county agency)[c]	Board[d]

Note: BOCC = board of county commissioners; CHS = consolidated human services, CHSA = consolidated human services agency.

[a] Numbers in parentheses represent the number of members on each appointed board.

[b] An advisory committee for public health must be appointed when the BOCC acts as the board of health (for a county health department or a CHSA including public health). G.S. 153A-77(a).

[c] A public health authority board that intends to pursue federally qualified health center (or look-alike) status may have no fewer than nine and no more than twenty-five members.

[d] In the case of a public health authority that serves multiple counties, the chair of the county board of commissioners of each county in the authority shall appoint one county commissioner, or the commissioner's express designee, to the authority board and these members shall jointly appoint the other members of the board.

Source: Kristi A. Nickodem & Kirsten E. Leloudis, Consolidated Human Services Boards in North Carolina (UNC School of Government, 2025).

Table B.2. Selected Powers and Duties of Local Boards of Health

Power or Duty	County Board of Health	District Board of Health	Public Health Authority Board	Consolidated Human Services Board
Adopt local public health rules	Yes	Yes	Yes	Yes
Create policy for the local health department	Yes	Yes	Yes	Yes
Adjudicate appeals related to local public health rules or fines imposed by the local health director	Yes	Yes	Yes	Yes
Appoint the local health director after consultation with the BOCC(s)	Yes	Yes	Yes	No
Set fees for certain services provided by the local health department, as permitted by law	Yes	Yes	Yes	Yes
Prepare and approve the local health department budget	No	No	Yes	No
Set salaries for local health department staff	No	Yes	Yes	No
Hire and fire local health department staff (other than the health director)	No	No	No	No
Sign contracts on behalf of the local health department	No	No	Yes	No
Hire its own legal counsel	No	Yes	Yes	No
Construct or otherwise acquire property on its own for use as public health facilities	No	No	Yes	No
Sell surplus buildings, land, and equipment on its own	No	No	Yes	No

Note: BOCC = board of county commissioners.

Source: Kristi A. Nickodem & Kirsten E. Leloudis, Consolidated Human Services Boards in North Carolina (UNC School of Government, 2025).

Table B.3. Local Board of Health Member Term Length and Term Limit

Board	Regular Term Length	Term Limit[a]	County Commissioner's Term on Board Contemporaneous with Term on BOCC?
County board of health[b]	3 years[c]	3 consecutive terms	Yes
CHS board[b]	4 years[c]	2 consecutive terms	Yes
District board of health[b]	3 years[c]	3 consecutive terms	Yes
Public health authority board[b]	3 years[c]	No limit	Yes
BOCC (assuming powers and duties of a county board of health or CHS board)	Coincides with term as county commissioner	No limit	Yes

Note: BOCC = board of county commissioners; CHS = consolidated human services.

[a] The maximum number of consecutive terms that a board member may hold.

[b] Board members selected by appointment.

[c] Members may be appointed for less than a four-year term in order to establish a uniform staggered-term structure for the board. G.S. 130A-35(c), 153A-77(c), 130A- 37(c), 130A-45.1(d).

Source: Kristi A. Nickodem & Kirsten E. Leloudis, Consolidated Human Services Boards in North Carolina (UNC School of Government, 2025).

Appendix C. Comparisons of Local Social Services Boards

Table C.1. Types of Local Governing Boards for Social Services

Board	Organization	Board Members Selected by[a]	Director Appointed by
County board of social services	County DSS	Appointment (3 or 5)	Board
BOCC as board of social services	County DSS	Election	BOCC
CHS board	CHSA	Appointment (up to 25)	County manager, with the advice and consent of the CHS board
BOCC as CHS board[b]	CHSA	Election	County manager, with the advice and consent of the BOCC
Regional board of social services	Regional DSS (multi-county)	Appointment (12–18)	Board

Note: BOCC = board of county commissioners; CHS = consolidated human services, CHSA = consolidated human services agency.

[a] Numbers in parentheses represent the number of members on each appointed board.

[b] An advisory committee for public health must be appointed if the CHSA includes public health. G.S. 153A-77(a). There is no corresponding requirement to appoint an advisory committee for social services, though the BOCC may choose to do so.

Source: Kristi A. Nickodem & Kirsten E. Leloudis, Consolidated Human Services Boards in North Carolina (UNC School of Government, 2025).

Table C.2. Social Services Board Member Term Length and Term Limit

Board	Regular Term Length	Term Limit[a]	County Commissioner's Term on Board Contemporaneous with Term on BOCC?
County board of social services[b]	3 years	2 consecutive terms	No
CHS board[b]	4 years[c]	2 consecutive terms	Yes
Regional board of social services[b]	3 years[d]	3 consecutive terms	Yes
BOCC (assuming powers and duties of board of social services or CHS board)	Coincides with term as county commissioner	No limit	Yes

Note: BOCC = board of county commissioners; CHS = consolidated human services.

[a] The maximum number of consecutive terms that a board member may hold.

[b] Board members selected by appointment.

[c] When a CHS board is first formed, members may be appointed for less than a four-year term in order to establish a uniform staggered-term structure for the board. G.S. 153A-77(c).

[d] When a regional social services board is first formed, term lengths must be staggered: Two of the original members must serve one-year terms, another two original members must serve two-year terms, and the remainder of the original members serve regular three-year terms. G.S. 108A-15.8(d).

Source: Kristi A. Nickodem & Kirsten E. Leloudis, Consolidated Human Services Boards in North Carolina (UNC School of Government, 2025).

Table C.3. Appointment of Social Services Board Members

	Appointing Authority		
Board Type (No. of Members)	**BOCC**	**SSC**	**Board Members Appointed by BOCC and SSC**
County social services (3 or 5)	Appoints 1 member on a 3-member board or 2 members on a 5-member board	Appoints 1 member on a 3-member board or 2 members on a 5-member board	Appoint 1 member
CHS (up to 25)	Appoints all members from a slate of nominees presented by the CHS board[a]		
Regional social services (12–18)	BOCC of each county involved appoints 2 members[b]	Appoints 2 members	Appoint members to fill all remaining vacancies on the board

Note: BOCC = board of county commissioners; SSC = Social Services Commission; CHS = consolidated human services.

[a] When a CHS board is first formed, the BOCC must create a nominating committee composed of members of the current (preconsolidation) board of health and social services board, as well as the board responsible for managing mental health, developmental disabilities, and substance abuse services in the county. The nominating committee recommends members for the new CHS board and the BOCC must make appointments based upon those recommendations.

[b] If more than eight counties join the regional department, each BOCC appoints only one member.

Source: Kristi A. Nickodem & Kirsten E. Leloudis, Consolidated Human Services Boards in North Carolina (UNC School of Government, 2025).

Table C.4. Selected Powers and Duties of Local Social Services Boards

Powers and Duties	County Board of Social Services	CHS Board	Regional Board of Social Services
Appoint agency director	Yes	No, county manager appoints director with the advice and consent of the CHS board.	Yes
Help director to prepare and recommend the agency budget	Yes, along with director	Yes[a]	Yes, though BOCCs establish the amount or method for county funding of the department.[b]
Review certain confidential social services records	Yes	Yes	Yes
Consult with director about problems affecting the agency	Yes	Yes	Yes
Advise local officials	Yes	Yes, through the county manager.	Yes
Adopt local public health rules	No	Yes[c]	No
Adjudicate appeals related to local public rules or fines imposed by the local health director	No	Yes[c]	No
Impose fees for public health services	No	Yes[c] (subject to BOCC approval)	No
Develop dispute resolution procedures for contractors and clients	No	Yes	No
Enter into contracts for legal services without BOCC approval	No[d]	No[d]	Yes
Purchase liability insurance	No[e]	No[e]	Yes

Note: BOCC = board of county commissioners; CHS = consolidated human services.

[a] The CHS board plans and recommends the agency's budget (G.S. 153A-77(d)(7)) but is prohibited from transmitting or presenting the budget for local health programs (G.S. 130A-43(b)(2)) and does not approve the final budget.

[b] It is the BOCCs for each county in the region—not the regional board of social services—that must agree upon the amount or method in which each county will appropriate funds to the department for the administration of social services and public assistance programs, the county share of public assistance programs, and any recoupments following fiscal or program monitoring or audit findings (Title 10A, Chapter 67A, Section .0301 of the North Carolina Administrative Code).

[c] The CHS board has this authority only if the consolidated human services agency includes public health.

[d] If a BOCC has assumed the powers and duties of a social services board or CHS board, the BOCC has authority to contract with an attorney.

[e] If a BOCC has assumed the powers and duties of a social services board or CHS board, the BOCC has authority to purchase liability insurance.

Source: Kristi A. Nickodem & Kirsten E. Leloudis, Consolidated Human Services Boards in North Carolina (UNC School of Government, 2025).